DOWN FOR WHATEVER

Poems & Bullshit by Kris Kidd

Photos by Cameron Lee Phan & Design by Paige Silveria
Fonts Used: Times New Roman & Abadi MT Condensed Extra Bold

First Edition: March 2016

ISBN-10:0-692-56906-5
ISBN-13:978-0-692-56906-1

www.thealtarcollective.com

For you.

CONTENTS

"My blood makes noise. And I'm saying this now, because I have a strange gut feeling that it will be silenced someday soon."

First Blog Post: June 10th, 2009 // 11:32 PM

Eat nothing but teeth.

Keep your thoughts
        locked deep beneath
        doe eyes stained
        with a lack of sleep,
and wait
        for the inertia creep
        of the ones you dreaded—
        the ones who said it
                wasn't over.

You're their four-leaf clover.

Keep your thoughts
from
        spilling
                over.

Take them back.
Shut the door.
        Touch yourself
        on the cement
                floor.

MANTRA

Keep your eyes
          on the exit
and your hands
          on the cash.
Your body's just
          a used car
          that you've
c   r   a   s   h   e   d
into the center divider,
but at heart
          you're a fighter.

So draw in your fists
with your
frail morning wrists
          and step back
                    to the street.

You eat nothing but teeth.

Blood to the dirt,
    he hit the ground
        with a hollow sound—
        like a million dying crickets.

And the sky was so fucking purple.
    Violet.
        Violent.
Red lights came
before blue lights,
    cracked rainbows
        in thousand-volt flashes.

The night air held you tight,
    and just for a second,
the world was quiet enough
    for you
to hear the summer ending:
    a dead cricket symphony.

    The way you knew it should be.

VIOLET

5

Cigarette butts
      like flowers in the ghetto,
the kids on this block have been smoking for a long time.

Summer is ending soon.
      High school is just a
            halfhearted and hungover
                graduation away, but today
          we're gonna go to the park and get high.

KIDS, DRUGS, SUMMERS, ET. AL

Billy's older brother
      Danny got fired from the CVS
              down the street,
but not before he stole
      the keys to the alcohol cabinet.

Our hands are always full and we are always running.

We sit, hanging from suburban rooftops,
          and we drink milk from the carton.
      We share pipes and toothbrushes.
             We own the streets at night.

Kimmy says she's not so tired of the scene
      as she is tired of the boys in it—
          those train-track boys
with their small dicks
and their big egos,
        but still she fills her *Hello Kitty* purse
           to the brim with 40s,
      and dances dirty with the conductor.

We skip school and we ditch chores.
We haunt shopping malls
      and grocery stores.
    House parties grow dull,
but Amy's boyfriend is a dealer
and we find ways to pass the time.

Michael is dying of cancer,
          but he says that he's not so much
                    afraid of dying,
as he is afraid of dying a virgin—
                    of dying alone.

I tell him if I were a chick
          I would throw him a bone.

Our parents go to sleep early.

Sometimes,
we lie about where
we're sleeping over and we end up
homeless for the night,
          but it's alright—
                    we've got the park.
We sit in the dew and the grass,
          and we smoke spliffs
                    until sunrise.

We roll in the bushes by the parking lot,
our tongues wet with drugs, like dreams,
          and we watch the suburbs shake
beneath the weight
                    of our screams.

Summers like this one
will all bloom and wilt
     like flowers in the ghetto,
     like a garden untended to,
running on the commands
         of nature alone.

And eventually we will all move on.

Billy's brother will go to jail and Amy will have a baby.
     Michael's teenage funeral will be super boring
        and Kimmy will find
          a million other boys
            to dance with.

Years from now, I will pass this same park,
and I won't remember any of this.

Instead, I will feel something like a spark—
     a heat like August
        in a suburban town,
          and a desire to grow
    even when I know
I'll be cut down.

We're sitting in the living room,
our voices soft against the tension,
        and she's choking on words.
The flowers she brought
                are in a vase,
        my father's absent scent
still resting on my skin.

UNTITLED, 2009

"It will be okay," is a lie
        and sometimes I think
that lying is all we can do
to make sense of this world.

I'm crying hard in the backyard,
my breath hot from the red wine,
        and she's trying to fix it.
The card she wrote
                is left unopened,
        my father's final words
still dancing in my head.

"It isn't easy," is easy to say
        and sometimes I think
that the only thing we can do
is say really easy things to each other.

Life Lesson #101

You are only as deep
as the ashtrays you use.
You only stick around
because you like the abuse.

Your camera flashed,
        and you asked
if I would take off my shirt.

        You loved the vulnerability of children.

I agreed that night on your bedroom floor,
with its shag carpet scratching   **YOUR SHAG CARPET**
                        at my naked spine,
my bones aligned in the shapes
            of never-before-seen
                            constellations.
And the room was all stars,
        Polaroids taped to your walls
            in a galaxy of others like me.

Your house was not yours, but your late father's,
        and his pool
                was almost as shallow as I was
when I asked if you thought
                        I looked good.

Your camera flashed,
        and you asked
if I would vomit for you.

        You loved the enthusiasm of the broken.

11

I purged that night on your bathroom floor,
my lips dripping stomach acid
                        and a lack of attention,
choking on my knuckles
                in search of something
                                like purity.
And the room was spinning.
        We were both getting lost
                in the great big black hole of me.

Your bedroom walls were covered in pictures,
        and your shag carpet
                was almost as green as I was
when I realized I wasn't the only one
                        being hurt.

Sorry mom,

    and sorry God.

Sorry everybody

    that got in the way

        today.

I may be a bit sideways,

    but there's two ways

        to phrase this phase,

        and blaze the days

    of childhood learning.

My teenage yearning

    is a fire

    left burning.

APOLOGIES

It's been five years,

and I'm still hurting.

Five years down,

    my heart's

        still flirting

with the concept of soft steps

    and best-kept

           secrets.

And I can't beat this.

There's something beautiful
about the way he'll give you his lighter
        when you can't find yours.
There's something fascinating
in the way his beauty fades
        when you realize your lighter was stolen.

FOR A GOOD TIME CALL

He's a board-licensed superstar,
        a carpenter
                since 900 B.C.
He's the one your parents warned you about,
        the flip side to every golden rule.

Do unto others whatever you want.

His mood changes with the weather,
        but he won't show it.
He's empty, sort of.
                He likes negative space.

He's what your son always wanted to be,
        what your brother pretends to be.
He's the All-American poster child,
        tattered and torn
                at the seams.

He ate the apple, he built an ark.
        He let it sink
                (animals inside)
just to speed up the evolutionary process.

There's something frustrating
about the way he forgets your name
        when he's playing the crowd.
There's something charming
in the way he whispers it
        when you're finally alone in the room.

His name is etched into your locker.
        His number's scratched
                into bathroom stalls.
He's got a penchant for degenerate leather
        and the taste of copper in the winter.

The grass is greener on his side of the tracks.

His world is shiny and hollow,
        but he'll never say it.
He's a liar, kind of.
                He dives headfirst.

He's all the things he's most afraid to be,
        all the things he's tried not to be.
He's chasing all his nightmares
        to get closer
                to his dreams.

He built the bomb, he pressed the button.
        He watched it burn
                (the entire fucking world)
just to see what the future would look like.

Sunrise is starting to feel like a guilt trip.

I dance in the shadows
        of downtown at dawn.
I've got the mouth of a trucker
        and a heart like a fawn—
                shaky and unreliable.

NIGHTLIGHT

I'm a teenage nightlight.
I hurt but it feels right.

I'm so tan my teeth
        g l o w
                in the dark
when I hang from the rafters,
getting high on soft sparks
        and forgetting my name.

Nighttime's a game,
and I know how to win.
All it takes is a wink
and my sad Cheshire grin.

And I'm up late.
        I'm getting my next fix,
                performing celibate sex tricks
and jumping through hoops
for strange men in small booths
        at the back of the bar—
I've given up myself
and I've stopped counting stars.

Sunrise is little more
        than a reset button
and a pang in my stomach
that reminds me of hunger.

I watch the sky
        change colors
and it's hard not to wonder
        where the dark goes.

11:58 PM

I dive into your sheets
(Egyptian cotton)
because, obviously.

11:59 PM

I declare
that I am incapable
of loving myself.

12:00 AM

I only hold on so I can let go.

MIDNIGHT,
EGYPTION COTTON

"Look at his bones,
so vulnerable.
Let's take him."

Impressive, recessive,
I am deviant
and excessive.

I'm all the things
you hate to want.
I'm an idiot slave
and a sex savant.

"Look at his bones,
like rust.
Let's break them."

I am all rose-gold
with the lies
I've told—
pink and blushing
like a virgin.

BONES LIKE DUST

I do my best
to hold onto
the pieces of me.

>   *"Look at his bones,*
>   *they're broken.*
>   *Let's sell them."*

Let's see down the line,
all those things
that were mine
are gone.

And now I'm kissing
the waste of it.
I'm making love
to the taste of it.

>   *"Look at his bones,*
>   *like dust.*
>   *Let's leave him."*

This isn't the end of things,
        but it's certainly not the beginning of things either.
You're undressing for the hell of it,
                snorting dope for the smell of it,
and you're hurting yourself, trying to prove a point
                        that nobody is willing to listen to.

At sunset, you watch the silhouettes of palm trees
        claw at the dusty sky, reaching out into the haze,
and you admire their solidarity,
                quiet and unwavering in the coastal wind.

You tell yourself that something's gotta give,
                and you pride yourself on your ability
                        to wait.

This isn't a suicide note,
        but it's obviously nothing to write home about either.
You're giving everything to get numb,
                pretending that you're having fun,
and you're crying for help at a frequency
                that nobody is able to hear.

At sunrise, the palm trees rest on the skyline,
        black against the light, a trembling jaw of crooked teeth,
and you lust after their loyalty,
                steadfast and still in the brightness of morning.

You ask yourself when you'll learn,
                and the answer is always,
                        "Tomorrow."

The night I first hear
        that my uncle is missing,
I am chewing gum with the lights on,
            wide-eyed and wasted.
By now, he's already been gone
        for a while—
                months, or maybe years.

Not my problem.

MISSING

I'm eighteen and nowadays,
my family members are
little more to me than pictures—
stiff Polaroids from the seventies,
dried out the color of whiskey,
        and worms,
                and dirt.

A history of bad men,
        a lineage of liquor stores
                and toothless gums,
the men in this family
        all go missing
                someday.

Not me, though.
I'm better on my own.
I am building an empire
of prescriptions and bones.

At night,
I'm lying in a hotel bed,
        counting what's left of my stash.
I smoke a cigarette
        and I ignore invisible stains
        from the night before,
because they say the things
you don't know
                can't hurt you.

My mom sends a text at around 1AM,
        worried, asking where I am.
I choose not to respond, and I wonder
if she'll send a search party.

At dawn,
in my hotel bed,
        all alone with my bones,
I lie in invisible stains
        and I imagine all the places
        these sheets have been,
always coming back to the image
of whiskey,
        and worms,
                        and dirt.

There's a downside to bedtime. I live a sort of nursery rhyme.
Catch me where the city lights are still burning hot,
flickering against the wishes of dawn.

In the soft light of morning,
the sky outside turning light blue,
my answer is always and still:

"I'm fine."

"FINE."

I'll say it any way you want me to. I'm a slave to you at night.
I just need the cab fare from your brother,
a drink from you, and then another.

I need expensive restaurants. I need five-course meals.
I want to stare at the plate before me
and push it away as a power play.

"I'm fine."

When I get bored, whisk me away to elsewhere.
Keep me there so long as I am stimulated.
I want you to help me forget.

Numb me like you always do.
I want you to.
I need you to.

"I'm fine."

Pour me another drink. Buy me another meal I won't eat.
Catch me crossing my eyes at all of the things
I was once so deeply in love with.

Let's take the train at daybreak.
Baptize me in the shimmering tides
of the west coast at sunrise.

"I'm fine."

Dripping neon like a nightmare, I feel the most alive at night.
　　I talk too much, but there's a lot unsaid.
　　　　I've slept in a lot of beds.

I perch in downtown lofts, on rooftops in the hills,
　　and I stare at the city below me,
　　　　twinkling like bright ripples in cold water.

　　　　　　　　"I'm fine."

And when the city lights have all burnt out,
　　when the rest of the world begins to wake,
　　　　your nursery rhyme calls out to me.

Listless as a lullaby,
　　you say I'm fine.
　　　　You swear I'm fine.

　　　　　　　　"I'm fine."

"Under the influence, I am easily influenced. I try to keep my pants on, but some things are easier said than done. I love like a beaten child and I trust like an addict."

Blog Post: February 13th, 2010 // 5:08 PM

Dangling from the fire escape
with legs like ropes,
        sixteen years old
        on the fifteenth floor,
I am so tied down.

I've been hanging in the back seat
with spitters and swallowers,
        getting hollow and hollower,
                with every taste of defeat.

On the fire escape, floor fifteen,
        (all bleach blonde hair
        and methedrine dreams)
I let go of a cigarette
and watch as it plunges
                back down to earth,
        flickering filthy ember.

I think it's December,
but I'm not quite sure.

I've been running empty streets
with these bicoastal ghosts,
        making champagne toasts,
                with the world at my feet.

On the fire escape, age sixteen,
        (all high rise lows
        and amphetamine schemes)
I watch the cigarette fall,
that spectacular light show—
                relentless in its pursuit
                        of ground zero.

And I wonder
        if I will look as beautiful
                when I burn out.

GROUND ZERO

You're young. You're drunk.
You're staying up all night
              in hotels that don't matter,
          thinking about the range of sound
a dog can cover in a single howl.

These thoughts spark a
          certain sense of jealousy
in your angst-ridden teenage bones.

For days on end,
          you wonder why the cries of dogs
can be heard from miles away
          while you're walled up
          in this godforsaken hotel
              thinking about—
                    what was it again?

Oh, right. The dogs,
          and their howling.

You're competing in the Insomniac Olympics now.
          The electricity bill is running high,
                              your brain dry.
Your eyes twitch in the most rhythmic of ways.

You have always hated addiction.

At sixteen, you were all opiate sighs
                    and amphetamine highs,
the product of a painfully adequate home.

Crawling on your hands and knees
through wet grass,
          sprinklers in the park,
you were wet-faced and screaming
because the drugs in your body were making
          the liquid experience of bathing fun again.

HOWLING

The comedown would hit,
	and the kids would keep moving on.
Racking lines with a bus pass,
	down the block you had a fire
	in your new shoes
that burned brighter with every step.

Your tongue was numb,
	and you felt like you
		could move mountains,
but you knew that no one was listening.

Even now, young and drunk
	in this shit-rent hotel,
		you can hear the dogs
but the dogs can't hear you.

Terrible people doing terrible things.
    This shit is all my fault,
                and I don't care.

Raw and passionate,
            stale like my cigarettes,
    the sour cavities in my mouth
go out of their way
        to remind me that I am young
                and I am stupid.

"You're falling apart,"
            they laugh.

Their call grows louder every time,
        but I've got nothing to say,
and I've got thousands of strangers
        who are dying to listen.
They crowd empty streets,
            spinning and invasive.

They get too close,
        and I've never been
all that great with human interaction,
        so I stumble, light-headed
            and heavy-footed.
        I land with one foot in the gutter
and one foot in the gold.

And I'd really love to say
that this is the end for me,
        but I'm far too good
        at faking intelligence
to convince myself
            that it is.

CAVITY'S CALL

I know that I haven't
felt sorry enough yet:
        sorry enough for age fifteen,
for being a life-ruiner,
        a sinner, and a whore.

I know that I've never been
        sorry enough for killing my father,
and I know that I haven't been
                turned far enough
inside out yet.

I haven't felt the full weight
        of the world on my shoulders,
and I haven't experienced
        a fraction of the pain
and embarrassment I've put out
                into this great big
                        white world.

The cavities' call increases with age,
and as my teeth continue to rot
        to the beat
                of the summer heat,
they tell me that I lack substance
        and nutritional value.
They say I'm sticky and sweet,
        and useless
in the grand scheme of things.

"You're young,
        and you're self-absorbed,
                and you're dying,"
                        they scream.

And I let them.

You undress, alone in your bedroom—
        sultry and shallow, set in your ways
                from a very young age—
as though there were an audience
to applaud you,
        your slow movements,
                your small bones.

FAKING IT

The bedroom is dark. Your clothes lie
                in a small heap
beside the bottle of Nyquil you had for dinner.
        The infomercial on television is about sex,
                the blinds are drawn closed.
Outside the window, men are standing in the streets,
        as strong as they are fragile, as hard to touch
as they are easy to break.

        A boy without a father is an easy target.
A boy with self-awareness is a dangerous thing.

Tonight you're dreaming of cities in dust,
        staring at yourself in the mirror
                and counting your ribs,
your only concept of time a slow burn
smiling at you
        from the cracked screen
                of your iPhone.

You sigh, force a smile. You lick your lips
                in the mirror,
your small mouth dry and littered with teeth.
        A woman on television is faking an orgasm.
                Her lips part. Her eyes close.
Out in the audience, men are shuffling in their seats,
        as hard to read as they are easy to follow,
as unwilling to give as they are willing to take.

        A boy with weak morals is easy to spot.
A boy with strong will is nothing to play with.

Life Lesson #270

There's stranger sex
than sex with strangers.

He's the king, Midas,
       and I'm a lot like the color gold.
Mighty Midas molestation,
       my dark blood shines.
It's wet and rusting.

His is a heavy touch that moves
with every
     b r o k e n
            breath.
He doesn't take it slow,
       but I know how this goes.

And they say,
       "Nothing gold can stay."

But I never asked it to.

So I paint my room bright white.
       I erase my face.
          I erase this place.
I know that it will fade,
       that I will fade,
              someday.

Gold-plated and understated,
I am over-exposed
        and I am under-rated.
The sea monkeys
        and the heroin junkies
are all one and the same
       if you're playing the game.
Do you know what I'm saying?

And they say,
       "All that glitters is not gold."

But I never said it was.

EVERYTHING YOU TOUCH

So he tells me that this will all be over soon,
                    that I will be over soon.
And I won't ask him to take it back.
          For what its worth, it's an aphrodisiac
for the golden kings,
                    and the bronze drag queens
who wear the crown
                    of exploitation.

This is called the graduation:
          A departure from the days
                    of what I used to be,
from the wreckage of a life unseen.
          A broken child
                    come out to play,
running wild in the streets
          and getting lost in the fray.

Don't ask me why,
                    it's just that way.
It's how I'll die.

This gold won't stay.

Locked in his car, parked on Sixth and Spring,
a man with a camera and a poorly shaven face
tries to touch me at midnight,
tries to put his mouth on mine.

I am kite-high and cross-eyed, watching streetlights
change colors at the intersection
(you know, red means "no," and green means "go.")
and thinking about colorblindness.

I often find myself falling out of love with the city.

Locked in his car, I kick and I scream,
and the man with the camera
and the poorly shaven face
reaches over me to unlock the door
and let me out into the night
where I belong.

The walk home is a comedown,
when the trains have stopped running
and I'm left to my own devices.

All monochromatic, I am highly erratic.
I'm a mass of gray area.
Gray roses, gray violets.
I am neon sans color. I am sexual violence.

At 1AM, the corner of Seventh and San Pedro
always smells like flowers and bum piss,
and I have, over the years,
gotten used to this.

FLOWER
DISTRICT

"The scent of flowers is always ours,"
my mother used to say,
          back when I was smaller
and the world wasn't so gray—
back when I was untouched, and
          things still went my way.

I often smile at the thought of a smaller me.

A secret garden in the ghetto,
the flower district hides at night.
In the shadowy hours between
               dusk and dawn,
I am either too early or too late
 to see the flowers,
(to touch them, to taste them)
          but I can smell them—
                    and that's enough.

You know the feeling at the end of the day,
      when you realize you've done nothing worthwhile?
When you've made no impact on the world you live in
          or the people around you?

Every year about 98% of the atoms in your body are replaced.

You'll sit in your bed or in someone else's—
      in the backseat of a car,
    or under a bridge—
  and you'll realize
that the world is still turning.

THE FEELING

You're replacing yourself, little by little.
    Every day.
        Every month.
            Every year,
              rebirth.

Nobody is noticing.

I've got this red-hot demeanor,
    a dizzying determination,
        when I cover the rooftop
        in Marlboro ashes.

It reminds me of the time that the city was on fire,
    buildings blanketed in palm tree ash
        and early afternoon sunsets.

MARLBORO REDS

The sky turned gray and the sun turned red.
    You said it meant summer,
and I said it meant the end of the world.

You agreed to disagree,
    and I disagreed to agree.

And you told me that I would never back down.

You coughed up your smoke,
    and you said that I was, and always had been,
    the wrong child—
        a little vagabond that lives too young
and breathes too fast.

I had that soft sort of ignorance
    that could never last.

All around us
    the world was burning
and all I wanted
    was to prove a point.

I took a drag off your cigarette,
    the cherry red
        like a burning star,
and I told you
    that you were right.

And for the first time in a long time,
    we agreed to disagree.

11:58 PM

Moonlight has long since
been replaced by the hazy glow
of my iPhone screen on 5% battery.

11:59 PM

Finger the blades
of my naked ribs
in new age moonlight.

12:00 AM

Tell me that everything
will be alright
even if I keep making
the same mistake
twice.

MIDNIGHT, TWICE

Hanging, lonely,
out the back seat window.
I can feel it
        in my veins
                and in my bones.

I can feel it
in my father's clothes.

CALICO

It's a head rush,
a sort of happiness,
        finite and fleeting.

        Did you ever get that?

We're racing up and down
        empty ghost town streets,
light-years above the speed limit,
and I'm not even
        in my own body
                anymore.

Light-headed and empty-minded,
        I'm getting lost
                in my father's seams,
in my childhood dreams.

And here,
with my head
outside the window,
I can watch
        the stars move.

        I can watch us all lose.

I'm a lot like you,
and you're a lot like me.
        It's sad to say,
                and it's sad to see.

Once upon a time, like yesterday but further away,
              sleepovers were still innocent.
        Starless skies in the ghetto
                      were still orange with smog,
and we still basked in the guilt of sneaking out
        to smoke weed in the park after dark,
rolling around in the grass
              and the dew, and the dirt,
                            until sunrise.

Childhood feels like a fairytale now.

You and I, we're not so young anymore.
                      We're a lot less lovely.
        Your father is dead, and I mean, so is mine.
Your hands are on my throat and I'm honestly trying
              to find a good reason to ask you to stop.
But you're just a boy, and I'm a certain sort of void,
        and the bedroom is dark, so I let you continue.

We used to wander the city at night,
                      stoned out of our skulls
        and looking for stars that weren't there.
I used to sit on your skateboard and listen
              while you talked about your girlfriends.
Your room always smelled like weed and incense.
        Mine always reeked of cocaine and rotten food.

I don't believe in fairytales anymore.

GALAXIES

I only call you when I've been crying.
                      I let you fill me when I'm bored.
      The piece of you that loves a part of me
tries its best to hold onto the rest,
           but my heart is a thousand-piece puzzle
of a faraway galaxy, deep purple,
          colors blending together and impossible to place.

Those early years weren't easy,
                  but we had a lot of fun.
      Sometimes when I call you, late at night,
I wish you'd bring your skateboard over,
           the same one from those nights at the park.
I just want to sit on it before I sit on you.
         I want to remember what we were like
                  before we became ourselves.

Sometimes when I'm fucked up or strung out,
and I'm looking at myself in the mirror—
        which I do a lot—
                I can't help but think of my family.

Young and Californian, in the mirror
                I am a bronze-skinned statue,
somehow mangled and distorted.
        Think: Egon Schiele does marble,
                        does David.

It's even worse when I'm coming down,
staring at myself and wondering
        what (or who) I do this for.
The marble crumbles
        and exposes my insides,
shallow glimpses of some kind of monster.

I've got my dad's eyes,
                those big, sad addict ones.
They're always bulging and glassy—
        wet like I've been crying,
                and usually I have been.

I've got my aunt's thick skin.
I've got my grandfather's weak will.
        I've got the pursed lips of every woman
                        in my family tree,
unfaltering in the face of destruction,
        and I've got my dead uncle's cheekbones,
which I'm pretty sure he inherited
        from the AIDS epidemic in the eighties.

It's like I've been Frankensteined together in a hurry.
My hands jittery from the blow, I fall apart every night
only to wake up every afternoon
        in a fervent struggle
                to put myself back together again.

        In the rush, I lose pieces.
Monstrous in my marble
        and my loose stitches,
                I grow smaller every day.

1

The man with the beer belly and the receding hairline calls you trash
    when you are fifteen and going on fucked,
        getting high in your bedroom and forgetting his name—
            all swollen from the blow and spun like twine.
You say that you would be much better off if he killed himself,
                if he disappeared entirely.
    You regret your words for the sake of mourning.

SHAKY
TOWN

2

The man with the long hair and the soft eyes offers you a ride home
    when you are sixteen and going on extinct,
        drinking cheap booze from the freezer at a party—
            all whiskey words and vomit in the backyard dark.
You oblige, and he drives the forty minutes without so much
                as asking you to suck his cock.
    You forget his name in the morning.

3

The man with the beer belly and the receding hairline
        is your father, and he's been dead for quite some time.
    You said terrible things in passing,
        and you gave your all to forget his name,
                and you asked him to die,
so you decide that the situation is anything
    but your fault.

4

The man with the long hair and the soft eyes
        threw himself off the Golden Gate Bridge a year ago.
    A friend tells you this in passing,
        and you still don't remember the man's name,
                and you hate San Francisco,
so you decide that the situation is everything
    but your problem.

I like the flowers in the backyard
of my childhood home,
      dead because my mother
hasn't been paying a lot
      of attention to them lately,
and I like the smell of gasoline.

I like the taut feeling of fullness
when it blooms beneath my ribcage.
I like the strain that I feel
      in my muscles and in my bones
when I am bent at the waist,
         toying with my tonsils.

DOWN FOR WHATEVER

My agent says, "You should have toned up,"
and I close my eyes, waiting
      for the soft wave
        of hard hate
          to hit my small skeleton.

I like weighing myself when I'm sad.

I like a good sex drive,
      but, I mean, who doesn't?
I like a good sense of misplaced rage.
      I like feeling used,
        and I like being underage.

I like counting money,
      and I like having the last word.
I like club music, and B-movies,
        and I like being choked.

My father says, "You've earned this one,"
and I close my eyes, waiting
      for the hard slap
        of soft leather
          on my bare skin.

I like attention, even when it hurts.

I like people with weak will
    and bad taste.
It feels like anything is possible.
    I like the claims of small children,
      like Columbus,
   trying to find out what's theirs.
It's all so intentional.

I like solving problems almost as much
      as I like causing them.
I like the brilliance of swine and octopi.
I like the smell of come
   when I'm trying to hide it.
I like a good intention
   when I'm trying to fight it.

I tell myself, "You will be okay,"
and I close my eyes, waiting
   for the light onset
     of a heavy nosebleed
       in a bathroom stall.

I like getting kicked when I'm down.

And so I wander uptown,
unprepared and unmotivated.
   Street rats scramble
     beneath my feet.
I like finding my own way out.

Apathetic in my adolescence,
my heart is fluorescent. It flickers
   like liquor store lights
     in the ghetto.
I am open for business.
   I am into a lot of shit.

I'm down for whatever.

"They say you can't build Rome in a day, but I'm pretty sure you could destroy it in even less."

Blog Post: April 27th, 2011 // 4:05 PM

The desire to self-destruct is innate.
        It is instinctual like breathing.
I wake up with it like morning wood.
        I eat it like breakfast.

I carry it with me like a backpack,
        like I'm on my way to school,
                or some shit.
        It is stiff, and heavy,
                and ceaseless.

MOSAIC ME

In the afternoon, it sits with me.
At night, it sleeps on top of me.
        It carries me with it
        like I carry it with me.

My desire to self-destruct
is a one-night stand
on Groundhog Day.
        Fucking repetitive.
                Repetitively fucking.

It feeds on me, takes pieces as it goes.
        I am lighter with each passing day.
I step on the scale and I smile,
wondering where I've gone.

The desire to self-destruct
is the smell of expensive cologne
        sprayed over the stench
                of a three-day bender.

It is the taste of the stale Diet Coke
        that I mixed with vodka
when I ran out of Redbull
            on that Tuesday in June.

It is the sound of me asking,
        "Hey, so like, when's Father's Day?"
for the billionth time this month
        in a blatant effort to get somebody
to ask me about my dad.

The desire to self-destruct
is festering and unflinching.
It's a mosaic self portrait,
        shattered and screwed.

                Me, but not me.

It is crying on the dance floor.
It is laughing during group sessions.

It's losing sight of the world
        when there's nothing left to look at.

Like a backpack, it is heavy.
    Like morning wood,
            it is ready to fuck.

Young and stupid, my food is placed
in a napkin on my lap more often
than it is on a plate.

I can't explain it.
Yes I can, actually.
I just don't want to.

It's the nature of the experience.
I talk like my mother walks
and I walk like my father talked.

I'm not making any sense, am I?

It's all such an effort.
My lighter or yours,
it makes no difference anymore.

You preach cleanliness,
so I try to keep my room clean,
but I feel no closer to God,
and I guess that's okay
because he doesn't know
who he's fucking with anyway.

My jeans are black and eternally torn.
I keep my outsides
the same as my insides.
I leave no room for confusion,
so you can't say that you didn't know
what was coming all along.

My slurred speech isn't from
            one or nine drinks too many,
                        it's from my father.

I sound a little crazy, don't I?

I get butterflies in my stomach
            when I stand a little too close to the edge,
and sometimes I wish that you could see them,
            but like me,
                        they're poorly drawn.
I sleep with the lights on.

All I ever wanted was for you
to bury your face in the hollow space
between my collarbones and say,
            "It's alright, kid. I understand you.
                        This too shall pass."

But I guess we're avoiding
that one at all costs.

All I ever wanted was for you
to bury your fist in the sunken space
between my cheekbones and say,
            "Kid, you don't know shit about shit.
                        You're gonna destroy everything."

But it seems as though
I've already repeated these lines
more than enough times in my own mind.

My lips are chapped, and my fingernails
            are always bitten and shit.
It's a lot like the way my mother walks,
and it's a lot like the way my father talked:
            inherently non-cognitive
                        and intentionally apathetic.

I'm not bilingual,
            but I am fluent in therapists' jargon.

Motel 6 leaves the light on, so I think I'll stay there.
            That way someone else
                        will have to keep the room clean,
and I can watch the seams of my black jeans
                        rip and tear in peace.

There, I'll keep the butterflies in a jar.
            I'll bury my own face in my chest,
                        and maybe then I'll understand.
I'll call my dead father long distance.
                        I'll call him collect.

I'll use the lighter I stole from you
to burn the place down
when I'm finished.

It's 4AM and we're on a bed at the Standard hotel,
        (the one on Sunset, not on Flower)
    just me, the producer,
                and the beer.

"You're a beautiful boy," the producer half-smiles.
    He's a little bit drunk.
                He has a wife and a child.

THE PRODUCER

I am young and fluorescent,
            shining in my new clothes.
        Drinking his beer,
I am God when the door's closed.

"I know," I smirk.
    This is a certain line of work,
spending the money of others.

Alight and alive, I am lucent like fireflies,
    lucid like my dreams. I am in control.
And I wonder if his wife knows
        where all the money goes—
            all the bars, and the boys,
and those shiny new clothes.

I rummage through my brain,
        (oh God, it's such a mess)
searching through my inventory,
        (oh God, where did it go?)
and I keep receiving error messages.

        This page is not loading.
        Try to reconnect?

In the disconnect, I watch him undress,
        and I say that I am late for elsewhere.

They say God is vengeful, but I get off on guilt.
       I get high on new clothes,
            and all the milk that I've spilt.

      Error Message #274:
      "Can't find God."

I've grown familiar with the feeling
           of watching grown men beg like dogs.
A Pavlovian twink, I give a smile and wink,
             and I shut the door behind me.

At 5AM, a frail God scrapes the halls
       of a hotel he knows all too well,
carrying with him
           the things he won't sell.

Hallways become lobbies.
       Bad habits become bad hobbies.
I watch the sun rise on Sunset,
         and I wonder
            where my heart went.

And I guess
      I've been bleeding for a while,
      running with the Friday crowd.

I've got knots in my bones,
      and I've got knots
      in my hair.
I've got cheap cigarettes,
      and I've got friends
      to spare.

I hate sleeping alone.

The Friday crowd
      takes flight in
the absence of sunlight,
circling the skyline
        at dusk
      like a cloud
of vampire bats.

There's Ritalin, Dexedrine,
      shooting stars,
      and Methylin.
A bag of bones,
I'm scary thin—
      faceless
like the mannequins
      in windows
        on Rodeo.

And I guess
      I've been dying for a while,
      living with the Friday crowd.

FRIDAY CROWD

I snort coke downtown.
I smoke dope
on the coast.
I live like a skeleton,
and I dress like
a ghost.

I hate telling the truth.

The Friday crowd
gets high in
the presence of moonlight,
fiending for light,
love, and dust
like an eclipse
of dying moths.

There's Roxanol, Demerol,
bright strobe lights,
and Adderall.
A piece of ass,
I've lost it all—
nameless
like the movie stars
on billboards
in the ghetto.

I gave them everything I had,
and I guess it feels
alright.
I gave them my body,
and they use it
every night.

Life Lesson #367

My closet looks
a lot like your closet.
Mostly because
I stole all of your shit.

There is a party, impromptu and small.
  There is an apartment on a hill with a great big balcony.
      It groans beneath the weight of us.
      Small icebergs melt in my red cup.
Inside, a bottle of beer is dropped on the hardwood floor.

I'll get it.
                                    Somebody says this.

There is a girl inside, her eyes wide and hollow.
  There is a darkness in her mouth that looks familiar.
      It swells between the two of us.
      Smeared lipstick, she smiles like a clown.
In the apartment, we dance to a love song that we both hate.

A boy in the room is wearing tight jeans. The boy is in a band.
              There is a guitar in the apartment also.
It's so hard not to be fascinated by the broken, to remember
      that a boy with a sad smile and a pretty face
          is not the boy that you should fall in love with.

Spin the bottle.
                                    Somebody suggests this.

I kiss the girl with the hollow eyes.
  Blood red, I kiss the clown and I become the clown.
          Her makeup tastes the way I feel.
      A ring of lipstick, a ring of fire. I burn willingly.
In the moment, we are a circus— a tent of lips and teeth.

When the circus ends, she leans over and she kisses the boy,
          the one in the band and the tight jeans.
My mouth stained red and my eyes stained green, I watch.
      I have always wanted to be the boy
          who could kiss with his eyes closed.

Are you okay?

Somebody asks this.

The air in the room is stagnant, heavy with the smell of us.
The world outside is still happening also.
It's so easy to get caught up in the realm of yourself, to forget
that there are things bigger than sad boys and beautiful girls.
But there is something inside of me, empty and wanting.
There is a weakness in the way that I kiss the boy,
the one in the band and the tight jeans.
My eyes locked on hers and my mouth locked in his,
he kisses me back and I keep my eyes open.

The boy becomes the clown.

I lick his tongue out of spite.

Nowadays,
         I deceive myself
                  in the strangest ways.

I'm a stumbling scarecrow
made of my own last straws.
         I often find myself
lighting fires downtown,
burning all the bridges
                  I stand on.

CHILDHOOD XR

My therapist asks
about my childhood,
and I tell her that I had
a Mickey mouth.

I always smiled big
         for the pictures;
skinny little bones
         and pixie dust pheromones,
I had young bedroom eyes
and I had no way out.

I was an emotionless bull
in my own emotional china shop.
I often found myself crying
in my bedroom, and trashing
         all of my own
                  belongings.

And his was
a time-released touch.
       It was a little too much
       to comprehend,
            so I pretend
I didn't feel him
in my bones
until long after
       I had swallowed him.

My therapist asks
about my youth,
and I say it's hard
to tell the truth.

I don't recognize the boy
       in the pictures;
shimmering wet
       in an emotional drought,
I had three black eyes
and a cartoon mouth.

Always out to play,
       I deceive myself
            in the strangest ways.

You have always been in love with the nuanced neon
        of shimmering puddles in a liquor store parking lot
on a rainy night, like rainbows in the dark—
                shallow reflections of a boy
whose life has been spent wondering
                when his father will come home.

You burn bright and you burn hard,   **WIDE RIVER,**
        like a fire in a dumpster,   **WIDE MOUTH**
                and nobody is so worried
about you burning as they are worried about the fire spreading.

It's a lot like the feeling of watching somebody get dressed
        in the morning, or in the afternoon. Pants around the ankles
                and small slivers of hard light, cigarette smoke
dancing through the blackout blinds—
        It's a lot like the permanence of a closed door.

Alone in your bedroom,
        a box of red wine or a bottle of gin
                makes no tangible difference.
All you've ever wanted is to sleep without the nightmares.

You trace the tributaries of veins in a man's forearms
        while he gropes you in the passenger seat of a parked car
on a sunny day like your life depends on it—
                giving your absolute all
to make sure this man knows
                you will die for him.

It's a lot like the feeling of watching somebody overdose
        at dusk, or at night. Dirty needles on the mattress
                and dark streams of light blood, lines of coke
resting on mirrors and on bookshelves—
        It's a lot like the transience of an open window.

You give the shirt off your back, no questions asked, and you stand
        alone at the cavernous mouth of your suburban closet—
your entire life spent wondering
                where your clothes went.

A giant on the city skyline,
my father was an unfinished skyscraper
sipping warm Bud Light and ashing
filterless cigarettes all over town.

When I turned sixteen,
            I tore him down.

A 98-pound wrecking ball,
all angry and scary small,
        I demolished him
        with the intention
of building something
        of my very own
                in his absence.

In the morning,
I marveled at his negative space,
        at the pieces of him
                all over the place.

I am seventeen now,
and I rule the skyline.
I am under construction.
It's okay. I'll be fine.

A 92-pound trainwreck,
all dirty money and blank checks,
        I piece myself together
        with the intention
of becoming something
        that nobody
                can touch.

ON GLAD BAGS
& VYVANSE

At night,
I marvel at my negative space,
      all the pieces of me
           that I can't replace.

I tower over downtown.
I stumble in the sunset.
I've got one foot in the ocean,
one in the ghetto,
      and they're both wet.

I dance over freeways,
palm trees, and three ways.
I get lost in the heat of
      my dead father's old ways,
           and I marvel at the view.

I like the way I feel
when I've got nothing to lose.

A giant on the city skyline,
I am an unfinished skyscraper
chugging Moscato in the daylight,
      and waiting for the day
      that I'll be torn down, too.

11:58 PM

Maybe if you'd fuck me
just a little bit harder,
I'd be able to see stars.

It's not working.
Choke me.

11:59 PM

Pin me down, I'm a pinnacle.
I'm your broken centerfold.

The stars on the boulevard
are all dirty and stepped on,
but so am I.

You say you love the way
I keep you up all night—
love the way I moan
even if it doesn't feel right.

12:00 AM

Maybe all I need
is a lack of air.

MIDNIGHT,
CENTERFOLD

Lying on your back, the cheap motel bedspread clawing at your skin
and his hands at your waist, a sitcom is playing on the cable TV,
distant and indistinct. Or maybe it's a game show.
The remote is missing its batteries. The nightstand is missing its bible.
You're missing something too, counting cigarette burns
on the floral bedspread while he unzips the fly of his jeans.
You smile, and he leans in to kiss you.

CABLE TV

A round of applause from the television.
Either someone on the sitcom just told a joke
or someone on the game show just won a million dollars.

You breathe him in. Filthy polyester gardens blooming beneath you,
his hands on your face, a game show is playing on the cable TV,
fuzzy and inaccurate. Or maybe it's a sitcom.
He tastes like expensive cigarettes and cheap wine, like indecision,
and you try to think of a time when that taste was still foreign,
a time before you had gotten so terribly comfortable with it.
You sigh, and he slams you up against the headboard.

An abysmal 'Boo' from the television.
Either a couple on the sitcom just broke up
or someone on the game show just lost it all for trying.

You take all of him in your mouth and he slaps you, hard,
his other hand on your throat. The television is still glowing,
and you're still playing the role of the whipping boy,
so hopelessly in love with the things that hurt you most.
And confessions of love have always seemed out of place
when you're gasping for air, when you're begging for pain,
when you're missing something, unable to change the channel.

Summer 2009

I am building a kingdom of dust,
losing everyone's trust,
and I don't even know it yet.

It doesn't matter.

So dreamy, sitting on the cusp
of paradise during an avalanche
in the summertime,
too hot to feel the cold.

Spring 2010

The junkie calls it "Coconut"
and I smile a sort of sigh.
I snort it on the floor of her
bedroom on the west side.

I am sixteen,
bleach blonde,
and invincible.
A peroxide cloud,
I disappear on the ground—
a stain in the white of her carpet.

Ignorance is bliss,
but it's not as
blissful as hubris.
I'm used to this.

I break things for fun.

The junkie calls me "crazy."
And I sigh a sort of smile.
I sink into the carpet, and
I stay there for a while.

COCONUT DIARIES

Fall 2010

My therapist tells me
that I am experiencing dysphoria
due to the loss of my father,
and I ask her what that means.

I've stopped bleaching my hair
and I am brunette brown
(like dirt or H) now, but
I've got little silver hairs
that grow on my head.

My mother says that everyone
in my family gets them.

>   *I love them.*

They make me feel dead.

Spring 2011

I don't have
>   *a problem*
so much as I have
a hard time stopping.

Winter 2011

Late night at the Regency,
seeing things that only we can see,
I am surrounded by fake friends
and loose ends.

A man with puppy dog eyes
and a hanging tongue,
offers me a line and I oblige.
And he thinks he's got a chance
now that he's getting me high.

Dog man tells a joke,
and I tell a lie.

Someone drops a bottle
off the tenth floor balcony
just to hear the sound it makes
when it hits the bottom.

I'm familiar.

Dog man asks where I'm from,
and I can't find the words,
so I sit inside my head.
Bottles crash like bombs,
and I can't fall asleep,
so I drink myself to bed.

Summer 2012

Sometimes, I think to myself that
all you need is a lot of money
and a bad idea.

And I'm not rich,
but I am dumb.
I am mastering the art
of getting numb.

Having sex makes things better
for, like, twenty minutes.

It's whatever.

I'm a hurricane,
a storm, a natural disaster.
Daily life is a task
that I can't quite master.

I keep finding new ways
to get away.

Winter 2012

They say the world is ending
sometime in December,
(before Christmas, but
after my late father's birthday)
due to a faulty Mayan calendar.

    I'm into it.

I am going to throw a party,
and we will all dress up
as ancient Mayans.

Everyone will come,
all my good friends
and my other friends.

And if the world doesn't end,
(if the universe doesn't cave in
and the rapture doesn't come to
tell us how bad we've all been)
then at least we'll all be wasted.

Spring 2013

The world hasn't ended yet,
so I press on half-heartedly
in my kingdom of dust.

I snort coke and
I drink coconut water.
I think of drug dealers
like I think of my father—
never really there when
you want them to be.

    Paradise sucks.

Look at the skin on you, wrapped so tight,
                              like dirty cellophane on bone,
and look at the color of the sky when any man texts you back.
        Look at the words on the screen
and the ones in your mouth that you'll never say out loud,
                and pull a little harder at your plastic flesh.

The bedroom will always be dark by three in the afternoon,
        the dust on the floor length mirror
                                that you refuse to clean
will always beam the image of a filthy boy back to earth,
                and you will always be the boy in the picture.
Can you not see the plotline laid out before you
                        like another meal to be ignored?
        PCH only runs so far before you have to make a U-turn.
Your great big escape plans fold in on themselves
                and they lead right back to where you started.

Another mirror,
                another bedroom,
                                another layer of synthetic skin,
here you are again splitting yourself open in the hopes
        that a man on a white horse, or a brown one,
                (you could make any color work, really)
                                        will save you.
Here you are again with a mouth full of steel crowns
                        and decaying teeth,
                praying that someone will notice, and offer
                                to carry you home.

WHITE NIGHT

A man held the world in his hands once,
                              and he spit on it for shine.
            He offered it to you, and you declined politely.
You were tugging at the seams of yourself,
         trying desperately to be the sort of boy
                              who deserves that kind of thing.
                   But you weren't,
            and nobody can blame you for that.

You let him fuck you anyway,
                   the world still glimmering with spit.
         You were taking in the colors,
                              you were stretching the plastic.
You were trying to find a way to get rid of yourself,
                   but you were still left with your mouth.

The coral reef of downtown is alive at night.
It's a school of fish with no other wish
than to drown you, but still you swim along
with your glamorous grief and your two left feet,
dancing on the shoals of anywhere
that feels like home.

THE REEF

The beat poets and the graffiti artists, the models
and the photographers, your friends—
they're all out in rare form. They swarm
(all shiny like metal and sweet like fruit),
approaching all outlets in a hopeful pursuit
of something like stardom,
so eager to get somewhere.

A lick and a promise, a spit in the sea,
you've been biding your time
and waiting to see
how this will all turn out.

The coral reef of downtown is crumbling quickly.
It's a whirlpool of water with nothing to offer
but fun, and still you stick around
with your lovely despair and your bleach blonde hair,
clinging to the shores of anything
that feels like love.

The drug dealers and the starfuckers, the junkies
and the couch surfers, your friends—
they're all losing their form. They swarm
(all rusted like metal and bruised like fruit),
approaching all spark plugs in a futile pursuit
of something like happiness,
so eager to feel something.

A drop in the bucket, a tear in the ocean,
you've been treading cold water,
memorizing the motion
just to stay afloat.

A balcony tucked somewhere in the hills, or maybe an exclusive party
　　at a pool on the rooftop of a hotel you've forgotten the name of—
　　　　　The specifics don't matter anymore.

Either way, you're high,
　　　　and either way, you're high up.

EITHER WAY

Up here,
　　the night is tangled and black like your junkie friends' sheets.
The city below you glistens in and out of focus,
　　　　smiling a mouthful of stainless steel crowns
　　　　　　　and decaying teeth.

This is a view that reminds you of you.
　　　　　This is a metaphor you had nothing to do with.

It's a sense of familiarity, a taste of cold metal clarity—
　　　　like blood in the mouth, or sucking on pennies.
　　It's the sound of your teeth crumbling
　　　　　　like the sidewalks on Seventh street.
It's the feeling of falling in love with boys, and then their fathers.
　　　　It's the feeling of hating yourself and yours.

The view is a bedroom dark by three in the afternoon.
　　　　It's you being a permanent fixture on the nightstand.
　　It's the smell of cheap beer, and expensive cigarettes,
　　　　　　and it's the half-hearted idea of going home.
It's the feeling of playing a game, and then losing.
　　　　It's the feeling of hating yourself for trying.

And up here,
　　with the world at your feet,
the entire city laid out and sparkling beneath you, it's difficult
　　to imagine a life
　　　　in which you weren't
　　　　　　so disgustingly attracted to it all.

It's a balcony, or it's a rooftop pool.
　　　　Either way, you're high.
Either way, it's a voice in your head that asks you to do it again.
　　　　"Repeat it for me."

"And I guess at the end of the day, you're just amazed that I can still stand, and I'm just amazed that I can stand still."

Blog Post: September 13th, 2014 // 9:37 PM

It is raining outside of Narcotics Anonymous.
        The sky is dark and sticky like black tar.
                I am smoking a cigarette and waiting for my ride.

In the movies, a boy caught in the rain,
        trembling beneath the sky and the weight of his pain,
                can look très chic
                        and "bad boy" sexy.

In the movies, the rain stops when they call cut.

That unfortunate boy goes back to his trailer
        and he wipes off his makeup and all of his troubles.
                He leaves it all behind.

The boy in the movies doesn't really have to walk home,
        and he didn't actually have to sit through an hour
                of "God, grant me the serenity,"
                        and "God, grant me the strength."

In the movies, God is an actor just like everyone else.

Standing outside of Narcotics Anonymous, I am très chic
        and troubled, shivering sexily and waiting for God
                        to call cut.

In the rain, a man with shaky teeth and a tattoo
        of a spider on his neck taps me on the shoulder.
                He asks me for a cigarette,
                        and I give him one.

I light it for him like they do in the movies.

SERENITY
PRAYER

85

On FaceTime once,
I asked you
        what you thought
                would happen
        if the world ended.

I asked you where we'd go,
        (but I think I was more worried
        about where I would go)
and you said
        that you believed
                in energy.

You said you believed
        that energy
                is all we have,
and you said it never stops.

I told you to stop.

I said I hated "forever,"
        the way it sounds,
and what it stands for.

You said it was beautiful, and
        I said you were wrong.

It was sunset in Los Angeles.
Outside my window, the sky
was pink like track marks.

On your end of the line in Texas,
        the sky was already dark,
                but I couldn't see the stars
                        in your digital bedroom.

CAMPFIRE

Airwaves between us,
        (you fascinated by the beauty
        of infinite space, and me fixated
        on the sheer terror of it)
I told you that I needed
a finish line.

        Existing is exhausting.

The miles of audio between us
fizzled and cracked like fire,
        and I think this is how
people used to share stories—
their hopes, and their dreams,
        and their fears,
                and all that.

I whispered static,
telling you that when I was younger,
I used to have nightmares about heaven.

You said I didn't need to be afraid,
                        not anymore.

And this was my cue
        to tell you I loved you,
                but I told you instead
that I needed to die someday.

        Forever is a really long time.

Parties in bloom on the beach at dusk,
        and fake friends, teenage tyrants
smoking dope in a bathroom
                    at the Tahitian Terrace.

Highs and lows wax and wane like tides
        in the passenger seat
of a stranger's car at night.
                    You let the dark in.

You build shrines
        for executions of innocence:
the first time you were touched,
        the first time you vomited from the drugs,
and the first time you fell asleep
                    with a lit cigarette in hand.

You grow bored of these shrines,
            and you abandon them
because you know for a fact
        that you will worship
                anything you kneel before.

Like God.

        Like cock.

            Like porcelain.

PORCELAIN

Waking up
in the bedrooms of strangers,
        in the arms of giants.
In empty college dorms
on the edge of the universe,
my fatigue is Ivy League.

I can't remember much
        but I can't say
                it was worth the wait.

Every day of my life,
I'm running around in the shapes
of letters
that spell infinity.

I trip,
because my shoes are never tied,
and it feels a lot like the way
that I drained every
metaphorical pool
        in the city.

Running on empty,
I've been touching the stove
just to feel the burn.

Coming to
in the bathrooms of airplanes,
        in the hands of losers.
In crowded hotel lobbies
at the center of the city,
my concerns are lessons learned.

I don't remember much
        but I don't think
                it was worth the pain.

THIS IS HOW WE LEARN

Every day of my life,
I'm swallowing stars in the shapes
of constellations
that have already died.

I choke,
because my tongue is always tied,
and it tastes a lot like the way
that I gave everything
I had
        to this city.

Choking on nothing,
I've been repeating myself
and wondering when I'll learn.

Life Lesson #427

The trick is to stop staring
at your own face in the mirror
just long enough to come to terms
with the concept of living
without the idea
of yourself.

It's cold,
        April in the loft
and my clothes are off.

The mushrooms hit hard after like, an hour,
        and I can't skate,
                so the half-pipe in the room
                        becomes a boat.

I float
        in my own sea
                of meaningless importance.

Asking no one in particular,
I call out for answers to questions like,
        "Why are we doing this?"
                and *"What does it mean?"*

Lights off,
I trace the colors in the air
        with my stupid hands.
I understand
a lot, and very little.

MUSHROOMS, APRIL

Eyes closed,
I can hear the dull hum
        of every freeway in Los Angeles—
        a unified vibration so strong,
it feels like I could move through walls
                if I really put my mind to it.

But I don't.

Instead, I burrow into a pile
        of vintage t-shirts on the floor.
        I lie on my back,
                and I contemplate the ceiling.

Through the skylight,
        I watch as the late night
                helicopters of downtown
circle above,
                searching for something.

An alternate
version
of me
lives
in every choice
I didn't make.

I want
        (so badly)
to touch myself
        without it
                hurting.

A better
        version
        of me
        lives
on the other side
        of my mistakes.

                        I want
(so desperately)
                to feel myself
                without the
wondering.

COHERENCE

Your sadness will not die when you find happiness, you know.
    Life will continue to be an all-day barbecue,
        and you will still cry in the toolshed out back.

All the wet t-shirt contests and the keg stands, all the chicken fights
    and the imminent signs of an elite and superficial club
        will remain. The vague humming of dragonflies
will still plague the poolside, and the soft light of summer
    flickering on the surface
        will still remind you of fresh blood.

Your past does not leave you when you choose to leave it.

The party will rage on
    and you will forage yourself
        from the pieces.

ON GETTING BETTER, AND ALL THAT

Your grief will not leave when you learn how to love, you know.
    Life will continue to be an all-night party,
        and you will still wonder why you were invited.

All the whiskey sours at the after hours, all the velvet ropes
    and the sinister smiles of bouncers and dealers alike
        will remain. The dull light of pale sunrise
will still haunt the west side, and the faint chirping of birds
    dancing at dawn
        will still flood your heart with guilt.

Your past does not define you the way you defined it.

The comedown will hit
    and you will pick yourself
        back up again.

STUFF I SHOULD HAVE SAID
WHEN I HAD THE CHANCE:

I love you.
I don't feel well.
I'm so fucking hungry.
I *am* trying.
Dad, stop.
What is Suboxone?
Is this what happy feels like?
This hurts.
Who are you?
Where are we going?
I'm sorry.

TEXTS I WOULD HAVE SENT
IF I HAD SERVICE:

These stars remind me of you.
Stranded out in Malibu somewhere.
Please pick me up.
I just want you to be better.
Airplane food sucks.
I don't know where I am.
I'm scared.
I can't do this anymore.
I want to go home.
It is so beautiful out here.
I miss you.

HOMECOMING

**THINGS I COULD HAVE DONE
IF I WASN'T HIGH:**

Gotten better.
Made an effort.
Finished school.
Saved my father.
Seen the world.
Gained weight.
Given a shit.
Made someone proud.
Cried real tears.
Felt real feelings.
Gone home.

11:58 PM

For so long,
I have based my ability to sleep at night
on the warmth and pressure of a person
beside me, on top of me, or under me.

11:59 PM

My white sheets are cold
and vast like oceans, and
the idea of sailing on my own
has always frightened me.

12:00 AM

I guess I don't mind drowning
so much as I mind doing it alone.

MIDNIGHT,
WHITE OCEANS

At sunset
　　　　on the west coast,
　　　　　　　the anemic shadows
　　　　of all your favorite buildings
　　　　bow their heads for you
　　　　　　　　indefinitely.

On the east coast,
　　　　from where you stand
　　　　　　　in the dark,
　　　　the Brooklyn Bridge
　　　　is reduced to strings
　　　　of light—
　　　　　　　radiant garlands
　　　　　　　over black water.

And that liquor store
downtown,
the one that never carded
when you were all bones
and a mouthful of braces—
　　　　the flag outside it waves
　　　　at half-mast
　　　　　　　in your absence.

BLACK WATER

Your therapist,
        your dealers,
        and all your fake friends
sink hearts in sync
        at the sudden realization
        that you belong
                to no one.

And all the drugs
and the lights
and the music,
        all the balconies at sunrise
        and the fast cars
        and the 5AM tears—

                        they were all
                        for you.

Parts of your life
will fall apart around you
    like hard mist from the ocean
        falls around your head at 1AM
    in the dark on a beach
you used to visit as a child.

You'll stand there
    with white flecks
    of foam
        in your hair
and the undeniably
    tense feeling of dread
        and joy
in your bones
    like you used to feel
when trying to fall asleep
the night before your birthday,
    or Christmas,
        or whatever.

White neon screen,
you'll glow
    beneath the light
        of a text message
        from a close friend
    that tells you to be excited
that you can still feel at all,
        you know?

White mist
and white iPhones
    and your white teeth in the dark,
you'll smile like you never have before
        because for the first time
    in your young life
    you can feel with substance,
        and without substances.

LIKE WHITE

101

Tangled in my sheets
and lying on your back,
    I watch you turn to greet
    the soft light of a sun
        that has just begun to rise.

Your body is still asleep,
but your mind is so awake.

I keep a box of photos beside my bed,
    relics of the ancient civilizations of me.
        Incarnations of self like
        all of the cities I've set fire to.
And I show them to you sparingly.

Photos of the life I lived before you,
    back when I had
    bruised lips and hips
        and knees that knocked
        when I walked.
Back when everything in my life
    was as habitual as breathing.

And I have never been too easily satiated.
    Things that take a little with others
seem to take a lot with me.

I've spent the better half of my youth
wondering why nobody told me
growing up would be so hard.
    A master at placing the blame,
    I've been running in circles
        and howling at a starless sky.

GHOSTS

I'm spending the final years of my youth
wondering why nobody told me
falling in love could be so easy.
         An amateur at real feelings,
         I am breaking down my walls
         and my thick skin,
                  howling at the moon in Texas.

I am far from that person now.

Rolling over in the morning,
twisting in my slutty white sheets,
         I pull myself closer to you,
                  and I am far nearer
to the person I could be.

It feels a lot like happiness.
It feels a lot like hope.

It reminds me
of the last glowing ember
of yet another city in dust
         at the end of summer.
Hot winds and habitual hauntings.
A spectral heat
         that sweeps
                  through the streets
before burning out entirely.

It's one of those things
you can feel,
         but can't see.

Like wind.

    Like love.

        Like ghosts.

And now we're driving toward elsewhere,
        cutting a soft scar
                into the desert's skin,
using the interstate as a perforated line.

Nicotine and stale young breath,
the beer we had for dinner
        still wet on our tongues,
there's a certain sort of religion
in the way we scream our fathers' names
        into the star-fucked night sky.

Quietly, a love song
        plays on the radio.
It casts a dim green light
on passengers' faces,
        glistening wet—
emeralds in our eyes.

We've got our whole generation
in the back seat of this old car,
running on empty
        and smiling still.

We are first-class holograms,
all mismatched maps
                and unmade beds.
        We're messy like our sheets
and the dreams in our heads.

Arms brushing in the backseat,
we've got Polaroids of sunsets
the color of lilac and fresh blood.
The color of deserts
        and beaches and forests
                and all worlds inbetween.

PARADISE

Soft scars on the interstate
and sunrises the color
        of your favorite crayons
                when you were young
and you still cared
        about things like that.

We are waking up on this side of paradise,
or this side of hell—
        we can't quite tell.
We've got our bags packed, and the music
        is playing, and there's not room
                        for much else here.

Made in the USA
Lexington, KY
27 October 2016